FIFTY THINGS YOU CAN DO ABOUT AIDS

Neal Hitchens is currently working on *Voices That Care,* a book of encouragements for people living with AIDS/HIV and those who love them.

Fifty Things You Can Do About AIDS

NEAL HITCHENS

LOWELL HOUSE
Los Angeles
CONTEMPORARY BOOKS
Chicago

Library of Congress Cataloging-in-Publication Data

Hitchens, Neal.
  Fifty things you can do about AIDS / Neal Hitchens.
      p.   cm.
    ISBN 0-929923-95-2
    1. AIDS (Disease)—Popular works. I. Title. II. Title: Fifty things you can do about AIDS.
    RC607.A26H55 1991
    362.1'969792—dc20   91-36217
                                                                    CIP

Copyright © 1992 by Neal Hitchens and RGA Publishing Group, Inc.

All rights reserved. No part of this book may be reproduced or transmitted in any form or by any means, electronic or mechanical, including photocopying and recording, or by any information storage and retrieval system, except as may be expressly permitted by the 1976 Copyright Act or in writing by the publisher.

Requests for such permission should be addressed to:

Lowell House
2029 Century Park East, Suite 3290
Los Angeles, CA 90067
Publisher: Jack Artenstein
Vice-President/Editor-in-Chief: Janice Gallagher
Director of Marketing: Elizabeth Duell Wood
Design: Nancy Freeborn

Manufactured in the United States of America
10 9 8 7 6 5 4 3 2 1

- In memory of *too many people.*
- To our heroes in the fight against AIDS: *thank you.*
- To *you*—for opening the pages of this book, for wanting to learn, and for wanting to *do*. Together, we *can* make a difference.

Contents

Acknowledgments ix
Introduction xiii

1. No Victims Here 1
2. When Santa Comes 2
3. More Over, Maxwell House 3
4. Put Away Your Pets 4
5. Don't Get Rid of Those Bags! 5
6. Money Talks 6
7. Something Smells in This Place 7
8. Lend a Helping Paw 8
9. Protective Equipment 9
10. Put Your Money Where Your Mouth Is 10
11. Tie a Red Ribbon 11
12. Brother, Can You Spare a Job? 12
13. That's What Friends Are For 13
14. Use Your "Condom Sense" 14
15. It's Like Comparing Apples and Oranges 16
16. Blood Simple 17
17. "Senator, You're No Jack Kennedy" 18
18. Gimme Shelter 20
19. Power Television 21
20. Wanna Ride, Sailor? 23
21. What's Cooking? 24
22. Something Smells in This Place (II) 26
23. Listening to a Book 27
24. Out of the Closet 28

25. The Envelope, Please 29
26. Have a Yard Sale 31
27. In the Bathroom 32
28. Share Love . . . Don't Share the Needle 33
29. Start Your Own Food Drive 34
30. No Laughing Matter 36
31. Be a Buddy 37
32. Involve Your Community 38
33. The Heart of a Healthy Country 39
34. Falwell's Follies 41
35. AIDS and Prostitution 42
36. Be a Hospital Volunteer 43
37. And the Verdict Is . . . 44
38. Call in Sick 45
39. Where There's a Will . . . 46
40. Alleviate Stress 48
41. Share Your Talents 49
42. It's My Party and I'll *Try* If I Want To! 50
43. Empower Yourself with Information 51
44. Fight the Disease, Not the People with It 52
45. AIDS at School: Class Project 54
46. Humanitarian Guinea Pig 55
47. Men: Keep Your Rocket in Your Pocket 56
48. Care for the Caregiver 57
49. Magic and Mayhem 58
50. Take the Test 61

Appendix A: *Safe-Sex Guidelines* 62
Appendix B: *The AIDS Glossary* 63
Appendix C: *Directory of AIDS Service and Research Organizations* 67

Acknowledgments

For their belief in and dedication to this project, the author would like to thank the following:

Mary Aarons
AIDS Project Los Angeles
Jack Artenstein
Gregg Barnette
Centers for Disease Control, Atlanta
Annmarie Dalton
Equity Fights AIDS
Christopher Esposito
Nancy Freeborn
Janice Gallagher
Mark Goins
Dr. Ralph Hansen
Bill Harris
Peter Hoffman
Aaron Kass
Lisa Kirk
Lise Wood

In June 1981 the Centers for Disease Control in Atlanta reported five unusual cases of pneumocystic pneumonia in homosexual men in Los Angeles.

~~~~~

Introduction

AMERICAN AIDS DEATH TOLL:
120,000 and counting

AMERICANS LIVING WITH AIDS:
approximately 380,000*

AMERICANS INFECTED WITH HIV:
1 million and counting

*AIDS has changed us forever.
It has brought out the best in us . . .
and the worst.*

—DR. MICHAEL GOTTLIEB,
who identified the first cases of AIDS in 1981

You've read the statistics. You've seen the faces of AIDS on television in your living room. The faces stare back at you, gaunt, harrowing, crying for help. "Something must be done about this," you say to yourself, shaking your head. And then you fumble for the remote control and scan the channels until you settle on a commercial for Ultra Slim-Fast diet drinks. And then you forget.

---

* This takes into account the revised definition of AIDS, expected in early 1992, as prescribed by the Centers for Disease Control in Atlanta.

You read an article about Magic Johnson. A lump settles in your throat. A tear wells in your eye. You are devastated by his tragedy and astounded by his heroism. "Why *him?*" you pose to no one in particular and everyone in general. And then the answer comes to you. "Why *anyone?*" Overcome with a surge of resolve, you hear yourself pronouncing, "Something must be done about this." And then you flip through the pages of your magazine. And then you forget.

~~~~

You go to lunch with a friend. The two of you exchange hugs, laughs, and eventually the usual gossip. And then the subject of AIDS (Acquired Immunodeficiency Syndrome) comes up. A friend of a friend was stricken with pneumonia and has been diagnosed with AIDS. The two of you shift uneasily in your seats, shake your heads, and mumble something about "the poor thing" and how "something must be done about this," and then you devour what's left of your Chinese chicken salad. And then you forget.

~~~~

You're at work. It might be a week later, maybe a month, maybe a year. You learn that one of your co-workers is a functioning, seemingly healthy person with AIDS. You are at first horrified, then afraid for yourself, and then, finally (and hopefully), compassionate. You want to do something to help this person. You want to do something to make his or her life easier. You hold the thought for a minute and then dismiss it. After all, what can *you* do? And then you forget.

~~~~

You want to do the right thing to help stop AIDS. But you work full-time and have an active social life. You'd like to "get involved" and do something significant, but you just don't have the time. And so you donate twenty dollars to an AIDS research or service organization. And then you forget.

~~~~

"Something must be done about this," you hear yourself saying once again. And then you say, "But what can *I* do?"

~~~~

Well, there *are* things that *you* can do. Things that you can do in your own home, at work, in your conversations with others, and in the spare time that you *do* have. Helpful things. Caring things. Simple things . . .

▶ Things to help yourself and your loved ones from contracting the disease.

▶ Things to help a friend, an acquaintance, or a co-worker with AIDS/HIV (Human Immunodeficiency Virus).

▶ Things to help improve the quality of life for people with AIDS/HIV.

▶ Things to help in the education of AIDS.

▶ Things to help in the research of AIDS.

▶ Things to help in the politics of AIDS.

~~~~

And, whoever issued the dictum that helping others had to be dreary and best done through gritted teeth? Whoever said that the subject of AIDS was something to be petrified or embarrassed of and talked about only in whispers? Actually, helping others can be the most rewarding and joyous experience of your life and this book is infused with that glorious spirit. As for the subject of AIDS being spoken of only in hushed or tentative tones, *Fifty Things You Can Do About AIDS* is willing to climb to the perilous peak of the publishing hilltop and shout out its messages until they resonate through the land. And, just what are its messages? Simple:

1) Something must be done about AIDS.

2) *You* can do something about AIDS.

Fifty Things You Can Do About AIDS is a handbook for anyone who has ever wanted to do something about the disease but didn't know *where* to begin; for anyone who has ever wanted to do something for people with AIDS but didn't know *how* to begin. It's a book for those who have the money but not the time; for those who have the time but not the money; for those who have only their hearts, minds, and hands to offer.

With this book "But what can *I* do?" will no longer be a valid question.

*There is so much that we can do . . .
and so much that we must do.*

—THE NATIONAL COMMISSION ON AIDS,
September 1991

1 BRUSH UP *on your AIDSspeak*

NO VICTIMS HERE

Someone with AIDS is *not* an AIDS *"victim."* Many people living with the disease are AIDS *"victors."* They are still alive, still kicking, and still hopeful despite numerous obstacles.

So what *is* the correct term to use when talking about a person with AIDS? Think about it. The correct term to use is simply *a person with AIDS,* or *PWA.*

2 *Give unto others*

WHEN SANTA COMES

When you're hanging up those Christmas stockings for Santa to stuff, nix the candy. Give individually wrapped condoms instead. Candy ruins teeth; condoms save lives.

3 AIDS in the office

MOVE OVER, MAXWELL HOUSE

The argument can be made that a coffee pot in the office is as essential as a copy machine. Nonetheless, for people with impaired immune systems, including people with AIDS/HIV, it has been medically proven that coffee and caffeine can be particularly detrimental. On the other hand, herbal tea can be of some benefit. So make certain that your office is equipped not only with coffee but with chamomile as well.

OTHER TIPS FOR THE OFFICE

▶ Do not set the thermostat at too low a temperature. PWAs are particularly vulnerable to catching colds.

▶ Help prevent the spread of germs by making certain that air-conditioning filters are regularly cleaned.

▶ Many PWAs have impaired eyesight and are sensitive to bright lights. What can you do about it? When feasible, replace the light bulbs used in your office with those of lower wattages.

4 When AIDS hits home

PUT AWAY YOUR PETS

When you invite a person with AIDS into your home, consider keeping your pets—particularly your birds and cats—away from him or her. Birds carry a disease known as psittacosis, which can be harmful to PWAs: cats carry toxoplasmosis, a disease that can be fatal to PWAs. Kitty litter boxes, bird cages, and fish tanks, all of which can contain harmful bacteria, can also be dangerous to PWAs and should be stored out of the way.

4 *Give unto others*

DON'T GET RID OF THOSE BAGS!

Forget the alleged Joan Crawford credo, "No more wire hangers!" Instead, save those extra wire hangers that you get from the dry cleaners and donate them to an AIDS service organization that provides clothing to PWAs.

Also, save those plastic and paper bags that you get from the grocery store and donate them to the local AIDS service organization that provides food items to PWAs. They cost approximately eight cents each—money that could and should be used in other areas.

Save the environment and help people with AIDS at the same time.

6 Money talks

(ARE YOU LISTENING, JESSE HELMS?)

Some people just won't listen–unless the size of their wallet is being impacted. So, make a statement with your money and be aware of where your money is going. For example, did you know that every time you buy a hamburger or an airline ticket you could be helping to re-elect such right-wing radicals as Jesse Helms? That's right, some companies use the profits earned from your patronage to contribute to the political campaigns of Jesse Helms, the agressively homophobic senator from North Carolina who has consistently led or voted for legislation that is harmful to–and against legislation that would be beneficial to–gays, lesbians, and people with AIDS. What can you do about Jesse Helms and his ideological cronies? Put your bucks where your beliefs are: be aware of businesses that either directly or indirectly advocate this brand of discrimination. Yes, these businesses have the right to contribute funds to the political candidate of their choice, but you have the right to know who *they* are.

According to the *Washington Blade*, the following is a partial list of corporations that, through their political action committees, contributed funds between January 1, 1990 and June 30, 1990 to the re-election campaign of Senator Jesse Helms:

American Airlines	Orkin
Burlington Industries	Philip Morris Corp.
Cooper's & Lybrand	Phillips Petroleum
General Mills Restaurants	Rockwell International
Hardee's	United Parcel Service
Kimberly-Clark	

7 *At the office*

SOMETHING SMELLS IN THIS PLACE

If someone in your office has AIDS, try to avoid wearing a strong perfume or cologne to work. Many people with AIDS have a heightened sense of smell and are vulnerable to sinus and other infections.

8 *In your spare time*

LEND A HELPING PAW

Often, people with AIDS are disabled in some way and are unable to take care of their dogs. Having a dog is often important for people with AIDS because many of them are homebound and without much companionship. However, a simple task such as walking a dog can be extremely taxing or impossible for people with AIDS. Or a PWA might be in the hospital and not have anyone to babysit his or her pet.

Do you enjoy pets? If you have a neighbor with AIDS, volunteer to walk his or her dog—it'll take just 15 minutes out of your day and you'll be making a real difference. If you *don't* know a PWA, contact your local AIDS service organization and they will put you in touch with needy PWAs and their pooches.

9 *The ABCs of AIDS*

PROTECTIVE EQUIPMENT

When your doctor or dentist prepares to do an invasive procedure on you, take some responsibility for your own health care. Be certain that your doctor uses the proper protective equipment: gloves and a mask. Be certain that your doctor has no visible open wounds. Be certain that your doctor uses sterilized or disposable equipment. Not only are you protecting yourself, but you are also protecting the doctor's countless other patients. Furthermore, you are helping to protect the doctor from possibly contracting AIDS from an infected patient.

Mandatory HIV testing of the entire medical industry is not rational, prudent, or cost-effective, but mandatory health-care protective procedures *are*.

10 The politics of AIDS

PUT YOUR MONEY WHERE YOUR MOUTH IS

Just as you would avoid AIDS-unfriendly businesses, you should seek out and support businesses that are AIDS friendly. These businesses have donated their time and finances to fight the disease. Buy what they're selling. Not only will you be getting a quality product, you'll be supporting a most worthy cause—with no extra price tag or effort. Naturally, this is only a partial list and is subject to change.

AIDS-FRIENDLY BUSINESSES

- Absolut Vodka
- American Express
- Anheuser-Busch
- Apple Computers
- Arista Records
- Bloomingdale's
- Bombay Gin
- Citibank
- Delta Airlines
- Fox, Inc.
- Hard Rock Cafe
- Home Box Office
- IBM
- Kellogg's
- Levi Strauss
- Macy's
- Pepsico
- Safeway Stores
- Seagram Distillers
- Sears
- Showtime
- Sony
- Toyota
- Universal Pictures/MCA
- Warner Brothers
- Woolworth
- Xerox

11 *Can we talk?*

TIE A RED RIBBON*

You saw it on television at the Oscars, the Emmys, and the Tonys. Has anything so small ever made such a big statement? What was it? A ribbon. A red ribbon that spoke volumes. Some of the biggest names in the entertainment business pinned a red ribbon to their tuxedos or their sequined gowns. Why? Because they knew that millions of people would be watching them on television. Because they wanted to say one simple thing: "Something must be done about AIDS."

It's fine and patriotic to tie yellow ribbons around our trees to support our military, but we all should know that almost *twice as many Americans have died from AIDS than from the Vietnam War and the Persian Gulf War combined!* It is also a fact that the size of the national defense budget dwarfs the budget allotted for AIDS, despite the fact that there is no war currently going on. There *should* be a war going on, and that war should be waged full-blast, full-throttle against AIDS.

So, at the next party or social occasion you attend, do what Kevin Costner did. Do what Cher did. Wear a red ribbon. And when someone comes up to you and asks you *why* you are wearing a red ribbon, you simply say, "Something must be done about AIDS."

---

* The Ribbon Project is sponsored by Visual AIDS, Broadway Cares, and Equity Fights AIDS.

12 *At the office*

BROTHER, CAN YOU SPARE A JOB?

Many PWAs have been either fired from or forced to quit their jobs. Many of them are relatively healthy, talented, and certainly capable of taking on a free-lance or part-time job. Many of them feel that they have little or nothing to live for. A job could help a PWA by providing him or her with needed funds, while also giving him or her a better sense of purpose and self-respect.

A prospective employer should be sensitive to the fact that the PWA will have fairly regular doctor's appointments and might be in and out of the hospital. Knowing this, if you are still willing to consider a PWA for a free-lance or part-time job (or if you know of such a job), contact your local AIDS service organization or advertise that you are seeking a "PWA" in the classified section of your local paper.

13 Give unto others

THAT'S WHAT FRIENDS ARE FOR

You're in a record store. You want to buy the gift of music for a friend, but you're in a quandary over what to buy. A little rock and roll, perhaps? How about the latest from Yanni? When in doubt, buy music that's not only good listening but is also potentially life saving. That's right, profits from the recordings listed below go to AIDS research. And what better gift can you give than the gift of life?

Red, Hot and Blue by various artists
Including k.d. lang, U2, Neneh Cherry, Sinéad O'Connor, Annie Lennox, Lisa Stansfield, Neville Brothers.

For Our Children by various artists
Including Paula Abdul, Bruce Springsteen, Barbra Streisand, Little Richard, Bob Dylan, and Sting.

Any new single by Elton John
Elton John has promised to donate 100 percent of the proceeds from every single he releases to AIDS research and service organizations for the rest of his career. Support Elton for supporting the cause.

"That's What Friends Are For"
Single by Dionne & Friends: Dionne Warwick, Elton John, Gladys Knight, and Stevie Wonder.

Also, support such recording artists as Madonna, Bette Midler, and Paula Abdul, among others, who have lent their names and donated their time to fighting AIDS.

14 The ABCs of AIDS

USE YOUR "CONDOM SENSE"

There is *NO* excuse for not wearing a condom during anal or vaginal sex. It is also recommended that a condom be used for oral sex. Use a latex rubber condom with a reservoir tip and nonoxynol-9 spermicide.

REMEMBER:

Gay men and straight women: Give him no love . . . *unless he wears a glove!*

Gay and straight men: Protect yourself and those that you love . . . *don't leave home without your rubbers!*

TIPS

- Keep condoms stored in a cool, dry place.
- Do not test condoms by inflating or stretching.
- Gently press any air out of the receptacle tip. Air bubbles can cause condoms to break.
- Use water-soluble lubricants. Oil-based lubricants such as petroleum jelly can cause condoms to break. In fact, the primary reason condoms break is because they have been coated with an oil-based lubricant.
- Condoms have a shelf life of five years and begin to deteriorate after two and a half years. Do not use condoms that have spent an eternity tucked in a wallet in somebody's back pocket.

MORE CONDOM TIPS

In 1989 *Consumer Reports* magazine named the safest brands and models of condoms:

1. Gold Circle Coin
2. LifeStyles Extra-Strength Lubricated
3. Saxon Wet Lubricated
4. Ramses Non-Lubricated Reservoir End
5. Sheik Non-Lubricated Reservoir End

The least safe brands and models according to *Consumer Reports* were:

1. LifeStyles Nuda Plus
2. LifeStyles Extra-Strength with Nonoxynol-9
3. LifeStyles Nuda
4. Mentor
5. Ramses Nu Form

15 BRUSH UP *on your AIDSspeak*

IT'S LIKE COMPARING APPLES TO ORANGES

Learn the difference between someone who has AIDS and someone who is HIV positive. Someone with full-blown AIDS has had severe damage to his or her immune system and has been stricken with one or more opportunistic, life-threatening diseases associated with AIDS. In early 1992, it is expected that the Centers for Disease Control in Atlanta will expand the definition of AIDS to include those who test HIV positive and have a T-cell count of 200 or less.

Someone who has tested positive for HIV has been exposed to the virus but has *not* contracted any of the life-threatening diseases associated with AIDS. The HIV-positive person has a T-cell count of over 200 and may or may not develop full-blown AIDS in the future.

16 *Give unto others*

BLOOD SIMPLE

You care, but you don't have the money to give and you don't have the time. What do you do? Give blood. Contrary to the irrational fears of some, you *cannot* contract the AIDS virus by giving blood. Many PWAs are in need of blood transfusions. First, be certain that you have tested negative for the HIV virus. Do *not* donate blood, sperm, or any organs until you are certain that you are not infected with the HIV virus.

If you are paid for donating your blood, why not donate the money to your local AIDS service or research organization? You will actually be doing *two* things about AIDS—not bad for someone who had neither the money nor the time!

17 *The politics of AIDS*

"SENATOR, YOU'RE NO JACK KENNEDY"

Register to vote. Then, do not elect politicians who demonstrate blatant disregard for PWAs, who express opposition to funding for AIDS research, and who advocate discrimination against people based on their race, religion, gender, or sexual orientation. If these prejudiced propagandists *are* somehow elected into office, write them a letter and let them know that their ignorance and bigotry will not be tolerated. And when re-election time comes around, vote and campaign to boot them out of office.

THE MOST UNWANTED LIST

Senator John Breaux (Louisiana)
Senator Richard Bryan (Nevada)
Senator Robert Byrd (West Virginia)
Senator Daniel Coats (Indiana)
Representative William Dannemeyer (California)*
Representative Robert Dornan (California)
Senator Philip Gramm (Texas)
Senator Howell Heflin (Alabama)
Senator Jesse Helms (North Carolina)*
Senator J. Bennett Johnson (Louisiana)

* They top the list.

Senator Trent Lott (Mississippi)
Senator Connie Mack III (Florida)
Senator Donald Nickles (Oklahoma)
Senator Harry Reid (Nevada)
Senator Richard Shelby (Alabama)
Senator Steve Symms (Idaho)
Senator Strom Thurmond (South Carolina)

WRITE TO SENATORS AT:

Senator _____
United States Senate
Washington, DC 20510

WRITE TO CONGRESSIONAL REPRESENTATIVES AT :

Rep. _____
U.S. House of Representatives
Washington, DC 20515

18 *Give unto others*

GIMME SHELTER

Many PWAs do not have a place to live. Maybe they were thrown out of their apartments; maybe they simply could no longer afford the monthly rent. Many of them are on a fixed income and can barely afford to eat, much less find a decent place to live. If you have a room or apartment to rent at a discounted price, contact your local AIDS service organization to get in touch with a PWA in need.

19 The politics of AIDS

POWER TELEVISION

In today's electronic society, the most effective way of communicating a message is through the power of television. And yet, over the years, television has earned a bad reputation because of the frequently mindless programming that it routinely offers. People call it "the boob tube" and "the idiot box." The nicknames are not entirely without merit.

Television covered the war in the Persian Gulf with patriotic fervor and 24-hour devotion. And yet we have a war going on in our own country in which our own people have died (120,000 and counting), and television has barely blinked. For the most part, the networks have succumbed to pressure exerted by hyperactive fundamentalists and right-wing advertisers by either dismissing or actually pulling programs that dealt with the subjects of gays, lesbians, and AIDS. An episode of ABC's *"thirtysomething,"* for example, created a furor when it simply showed two men in bed together. No nudity or lovemaking was depicted. Half of the show's sponsors pulled out, including Toys R Us. When the episode was slated to be rerun, ABC, fearful of losing more sponsors, replaced it with another episode.

What can you do? You can write a letter to the network executives. You can also start a petition, collect signatures, and send it to these executives. Let them know that (1) you will not tolerate censorship as prescribed by their advertisers; (2) you want to see more AIDS coverage on the network news: (3) you want to see more movies and programs that deal with AIDS;

(4) you are a responsible adult who can handle watching a program about AIDS or other gay issues; and (5) you can handle watching a commercial for condoms.

ABC
Daniel Burke, President
77 W. 66th St., 10th floor
New York, NY 10023

NBC
Robert Wright, President
30 Rockefeller Plaza
New York, NY 10112

CBS
Jeff Sagansky, President
7800 Beverly Blvd.
Los Angeles, CA 90036

FOX
Jamie Kellner, President
P.O. Box 900
Beverly Hills, CA 90213

20 *In your spare time*

WANNA RIDE, SAILOR?

PWAs are often no longer able to drive or are without a car. If you know a PWA who works in or near your office, volunteer to give him or her a ride to and from work.

Or, if you have a little spare time between 8:00 A.M. and 6:00 P.M. Monday through Friday, offer to give a PWA a ride to and from a doctor or hospital appointment. If you don't know a PWA who needs a ride, simply call the transportation department of your local AIDS service organization. They'll put you in touch with someone who needs a hand.

21 When AIDS hits home

WHAT'S COOKING?

You're planning a dinner party. One of your guests has AIDS. Will this affect the planning of your menu? You bet! Obviously, everyone has their own likes and dislikes, but the following guidelines are relevant to PWAs. PWAs are more susceptible to infection and are at greater risk of serious illness.

Beware of certain types of seafood: Raw shellfish, oysters on the half shell, raw clams, sushi, sashimi, mussels, and snails should *not* be eaten. All can contain harmful bacteria.

No raw or undercooked meat: Toxoplasmosis, which can be acquired through raw or undercooked meat, can be fatal to PWAs. Raw or undercooked meat can also cause listeriosis and salmonella poisoning.

No raw or undercooked poultry: Can cause campylobacter infection, listeriosis, and salmonella poisoning.

No raw eggs: Do not serve raw eggs, and avoid using raw eggs as an ingredient in homemade mayonnaise, hollandaise sauce, homemade ice cream, fruit smoothies, protein drinks, Caesar salad, or any other recipe. Fry eggs on both sides instead of cooking them sunny-side up.

No unwashed fruit or vegetables: PWAs are susceptible to picking up germs from unwashed produce.

No unpasteurized milk or cheese: Can cause campylobacter infection and listeriosis. *Pasteurization* means that the product has been treated with heat to destroy germs.

OTHER FOOD TIPS

▸ Thaw frozen meats and foods in the refrigerator or in a microwave oven set at defrost. Do *not* thaw at room temperature. Germs grow at room temperature and can make a PWA very sick.

▸ Use different cutting boards for raw and cooked foods to avoid cross-contamination. Plastic cutting boards are easier to clean than wooden boards.

▸ Throw away moldy cheese—do not just cut off the moldy part.

▸ Wash dishes in hot water—preferably in a dishwasher.

MORE FOOD

Can you cook? If you can't, do you have the time to deliver a meal? There are various programs across the country that involve cooking and delivering meals for and to homebound and disabled PWAs. Project Open Hand (San Francisco) and Project Angel Food (Los Angeles) are two such programs. Simply contact your local AIDS service organization to find out about similar programs offered in your community.

22 *Give unto others*

SOMETHING SMELLS IN THIS PLACE (II)

You learn that a friend is sick and has been hospitalized. The diagnosis? AIDS. Instinctively, you pick up the telephone to call your local florist. But before you call, consider this: PWAs are vulnerable to sinus infections, and many of them have a heightened sense of smell and cannot tolerate fragrant flowers. You're already being thoughtful by wanting to send flowers, so what can you do that is even more thoughtful? Simple. Send unscented flowers, balloons, or some other gift that will brighten a hospital room!

23 *Give unto others*

LISTENING TO A BOOK

Many PWAs have had their eyesight impaired by CMV (cytomegalovirus) retinitis and have a difficult time reading. So, if you want to give a PWA a book, get one with large print, or better yet, buy her or him a book on audiocassette.

Also, if you know a PWA with impaired eyesight who lives out of state, instead of writing him or her a letter, *record* your letter on audio- or videotape.

24 *Can we talk?*

OUT OF THE CLOSET

We're talking obituaries here. Don't let what are in effect your last words be a lie. Don't let what are in effect your friend's last words be a lie. Not a pleasant thought, but one that has rarely been addressed and that *should* be talked about.

Countless thousands of people have died from complications caused by AIDS and yet, according to their obituaries, they died of cancer, tuberculosis, heart failure, or some other "acceptable" disease. Altering the cause of death in an obituary only reinforces the stigma attached to AIDS. It serves to condone the theory that people with AIDS lived a shameful life and died a shameful death.

This is a terribly destructive practice. Until people "come out" about their AIDS status—in life and in death—many people will assume that AIDS is something to be ashamed of and something that does not affect them.

If you know a PWA, a person who is HIV positive, or a loved one or family member of a PWA, talk to him or her about truth in obituaries. In this case, honesty truly is the best legacy.

25 *The politics of AIDS*

THE ENVELOPE, PLEASE

Years from now, when history is reviewed by our descendants, our country will be judged in large part by the way it dealt with the AIDS crisis of the 1980s and the 1990s. Was it handled with compassion, intelligence, and expediency? Or was it handled with fear, paranoia, and propaganda? Was it manipulated by politicians to espouse their own prejudices?

The jury, obviously, is still out on this subject. But one thing is already certain in the battle against AIDS: a handful of our elected officials have stood out from the political pack and have made a positive difference.

Write them a letter. Let them know that you appreciate their efforts. After all, without them, men like Jesse Helms would be winning a war based on bigotry and hatred.

The following is a partial list and is subject to change.

AND THE WINNERS ARE:

Senator Brock Adams (Washington)
Senator Bill Bradley (New Jersey)
Senator John Chafee (Rhode Island)
Senator Alan Cranston (California)
Senator Daniel Inouye (Hawaii)
Senator James Jeffords (Vermont)
Senator John Kerry (Massachusetts)
Senator Edward Kennedy (Massachusetts)
Senator Patrick Leahy (Vermont)

Senator Barbara Mikulski (Maryland)
Senator Paul Simon (Illinois)
Representative Henry Waxman (California)
Representative Ted Weiss (New York)

WRITE TO SENATORS AT:

Senator _____
United States Senate
Washington, DC 20510

WRITE TO CONGRESSIONAL REPRESENTATIVES AT :

Rep. _____
U.S. House of Representatives
Washington, DC 20515

26 *Give unto others*

HAVE A YARD SALE

You'd like to donate money to AIDS research or services, but you're low on cash. Like most everybody, you probably have a lot of "junk" stored away in your closets or garage—old gifts you never opened or used, or old clothes you no longer wear. What can you do? Host a yard sale and donate the proceeds to your local AIDS research or services center!

On your next available Saturday or Sunday, set up a stand outside your house or apartment and peddle your wares. You might want to team up with some friends who also have goods to sell. It will probably help sales if you post a sign stating that the proceeds will be donated to a local AIDS organization. Clean out your house and garage, meet your neighbors, and enjoy the gratification of doing a good deed.

27 AIDS at the office

IN THE BATHROOM

Apprehensive about or afraid of sharing the office restroom with a PWA? You should know by now that you cannot get AIDS from a shower or bath, a toilet seat, or a wash basin. Insisting on using a separate bathroom only serves to propagate misinformation about AIDS. Of the one million Americans infected with HIV, not *one* was exposed to the virus by sharing a bathroom with somebody.

But bathrooms *are* a breeding ground for bacteria, and a PWA is susceptible to picking up *your* germs. Because of their compromised immune systems, an infection can be extremely serious to PWAs. What can you do?

▶ Keep your company bathroom *clean*. Not just superficially clean, *bacteria* clean. Use bleach or rubbing alcohol to sterilize your bathroom.

▶ Instead of using any soap that was bought on sale, use a liquid, antibacterial soap such as Dial. And wash your hands thoroughly with hot water every time you use the restroom.

28 The ABCs of AIDS

SHARE LOVE . . .
DON'T SHARE THE NEEDLE

Do not use I.V. drugs. If you know someone who uses I.V. drugs, warn them about AIDS. Tell them that one of the primary ways that AIDS is transmitted is by sharing infected needles. If you cannot dissuade someone from using I.V. drugs, encourage them to at least sterilize their needles with household bleach.

Put aside your moral objections to drug use: the prevention of AIDS is not about morality. Encourage your elected officials to support a program that would hand out clean needles and bleach in high-risk neighborhoods. A 1991 study concluded that the HIV infection rate in New Haven, Connecticut fell by one-third in just eight months after sterile hypodermic syringes were distributed to drug users. Programs like these could not only save the life of the I.V. drug user, but they could also save the life of everyone who he or she has sex with or shares needles with, as well as the lives of his or her children.

29 *Give unto others*

START YOUR OWN FOOD DRIVE

Your local AIDS service organization provides food items and toiletries at no cost to PWAs. A lot of these products have been donated by caring people like you.

You can help in a big way by organizing your own food drive! First, consult a representative at your local AIDS service organization and compose a shopping list of items that are most wanted and needed. Then go to your local grocery store, ask to see the manager, and get permission for you and maybe a few of your friends to launch a food drive.

Before the designated date, print a few hundred copies of the shopping list. On the day of the food drive, set up a stand outside the store and pass out copies of the list to shoppers as they enter. Encourage shoppers to help out by purchasing just an item or two from the list and leaving them with you as they leave. At the end of the day, deliver the goods to your local AIDS service organization, and enjoy the satisfaction of knowing that you have done something about AIDS and have involved your community as well.

OTHER FOOD-DRIVE TIPS

▶ Start a food drive at your office. Ask your employer to match the amount of food items donated by the employees.

▶ Host a dinner party at your house. When your guests ask the mandatory question, "What can I bring?," surprise them: instead of telling them to prepare a certain dish, ask them to bring all of the *ingredients* needed to make the dish. Then donate the goods to your local AIDS service organization.

▶ Be sure that all items donated are canned or properly packaged.

30 *Can we talk?*

NO LAUGHING MATTER

Your friend or co-worker tells an AIDS joke. Everybody laughs nervously. What do you do? You should inform the joke-teller in a calm and rational manner that AIDS jokes are not funny, nor are they in fashion. Tell him or her that AIDS is no laughing matter. As long as people feel that they can mask their bigotry by making a joke—and get away with it—they will continue to spread that bigotry. If you laugh along with the others or if you don't say anything, you are in effect condoning the bigotry and ignorance that prompts an AIDS joke.

We have gotten Andrew Dice Clay and Sam Kinison to stop telling AIDS jokes. Now it's time to get your friends and coworkers to stop spreading the same kind of ignorance.

31 *In your spare time*

BE A BUDDY

You've heard about being a Big Brother to a young child in need of companionship and guidance. The same principle applies to being a "Buddy" to a PWA. A PWA is often alone and forgotten. As a Buddy, you can visit a PWA and perhaps take him or her for a drive or to a movie. Most important, though, you will be a companion, someone the PWA can talk to. Call your local AIDS service organization for information and training on how to become a Buddy.

OTHER TIPS

▶ If you are without transportation or are otherwise immobile, contact your AIDS service organization about becoming a phone Buddy.

▶ Become a pen pal, or mail Buddy, to a PWA.

32 *Give unto others*

INVOLVE YOUR COMMUNITY

Don't let people *not* get involved. AIDS is a communicable disease and a community problem. There is something that everyone can do.

▶ Get your local video store to host a video-thon, a day in which all of the proceeds from rented videos go to an AIDS research or service organization. Not only will this help PWAs, it is also good public relations for the video store.

▶ Get your local hair salon to host a cut-a-thon, a day in which all of the proceeds from haircuts go to an AIDS research or service organization.

▶ Get your local bowling alley to host a bowl-a-thon . . .

You get the idea. Remember: every person, every business can do *something*.

33 The politics of AIDS

THE HEART OF A HEALTHY COUNTRY

One dramatic thing that AIDS has done is to graphically illustrate the health-care problem in the United States. Private health insurance companies want to insure only the healthy. If you are lucky enough to get approved for a policy, your insurance company has the power to restrict the coverage. For instance, if you are susceptible to getting tonsillitis, your insurance policy might cover everything *but* tonsillitis.

Insurance companies are doing everything they can to *not* insure people who are at high risk for AIDS. Some companies refuse to cover an unmarried man in his 30s (particularly if he names another non-blood-related man as his beneficiary). Some companies refuse to cover a man who works in a hair salon or a man who works as an interior designer. Some companies have set a $50,000 or less limit that they will pay for a PWA; as most everyone knows, $50,000 will cover about one week in the hospital and little more.

One of the top priorities of any civilized society (if not *the* top priority) should be to provide health care to its people—particularly to the people who need it the most. This is decidedly *not* happening in the United States, the wealthiest country in the world.

What can you do? Write your senators and congressional representatives and let them know that the time for a national health-care policy is *now*. And when election time comes around, demand to know what each candidate plans to *do* about a national health-care policy.

Demand a national health-care policy, not just for PWAs but for everybody in need of health care *now* or in the near future.

Health care insurance companies are in the business of providing health care, yet when somebody becomes sick, the insurance company balks. Likewise, there are medical professionals and hospitals out there who refuse to treat PWAs. They are in the business of providing medical care to people who are sick, yet because of their own irrational fears or prejudices they opt not to treat PWAs. Whether or not these professionals or hospitals have the right to refuse treatment to PWAs, *they should still be sent this message:* If they refuse to treat, at their own whim, certain individuals with certain illnesses, they can be certain that they will not have your support or business. After all, if they refuse to treat a PWA, what's to prevent them from refusing to treat *you* at some point in the future?

WRITE TO SENATORS AT:

Senator _____
United States Senate
Washington, DC 20510

WRITE TO CONGRESSIONAL REPRESENTATIVES AT:

Rep. _____
U.S. House of Representatives
Washington, DC 20515

34 *Can we talk?*

FALWELL'S FOLLIES

Many churches have responded to the AIDS crisis with love and compassion. Many have not. It is ludicrous and seemingly criminal that certain churches preach *against* the use of the one real, rational defense we have against the spread of the AIDS virus: the condom.

Who knows how many thousands of lives have been taken and are being taken daily because of this policy of some churches?

What can you do? Talk about AIDS in your church and share your knowledge with your fellow church members. If they tell you that AIDS is God's wrath against homosexuals, ask them why, then, is AIDS taking the lives of heterosexual men and women and children by the thousands? Ask them if cancer, heart disease, and tuberculosis are other examples of God's wrath. Remind them that AIDS is a disease and that it is not up to them to judge their fellow man—that is God's domain, and His alone. Tell them that your God is a loving one who preaches compassion, *not* genocide.

35 *The politics of AIDS*

AIDS AND PROSTITUTION

Don't kid yourself. One primary way that AIDS is being spread is through prostitution. It would be safe and wise to assume that every prostitute is a potential carrier of the AIDS virus. After all, the virus is spread mostly by unsafe sex and I.V. drug use, both of which come with the territory of prostitution. And do you know who pays for having sex with prostitutes? Primarily heterosexual (and oftentimes married) men who could then pass the infection to any—perhaps all—of their subsequent sexual partners.

What can you do? Again, set aside your personal ideas about morality. Prostitution will never disappear. Campaign to legalize, tax, and *license* prostitution. The funds raised by taxes can go to AIDS research. Before a prostitute can obtain a license, he or she must test negative for the HIV antibody. A study conducted in Germany showed that of those prostitutes who tested positive for HIV, only 1 percent were licensed, and 20 percent were unlicensed. Obviously, this won't solve the problem of prostitution, but it would be a big step toward stopping the transmission of the AIDS virus. And, obviously, if you are going to engage in sex with a prostitute, have safe sex and safe sex *only*—use condoms.

36 *In your spare time*

BE A HOSPITAL VOLUNTEER

Many hospitalized PWAs are without friends or family. They're alone and scared. What can you do? Become a hospital volunteer. It'll take only a few hours a week, and you can make a real difference in the lives of PWAs. By being a hospital volunteer, you can help PWAs both emotionally and practically. You can provide companionship and a sympathetic ear. You can inform them about various AIDS service organizations and support groups that could improve the quality of their lives. Most important, though, you can *listen* to what they have to say.

Contact your local AIDS service organization and find out when the next hospital-volunteer training class begins.

Even if you decide not to become a hospital volunteer, you can still make a difference in the quality of the lives of hospitalized PWAs. You can donate books, used video- and audiotapes, or unused greeting cards and postcards to the AIDS ward of your local hospital.

37 BRUSH UP on your AIDSspeak

AND THE VERDICT IS . . .

As "No Victims Here," (see page 1) states, PWAs are *not* victims. Further, don't make the common mistake of referring to a child with AIDS as "an innocent victim." Most everyone with the disease did not bring it upon themselves, nor are they guilty of any crime. Using the term *innocent victim* implies that others with the disease are somehow guilty or immoral. It is a term propagated by religious fanatics and right-wing politicians.

38 AIDS in the office

CALL IN SICK

You wake up in the morning with a cold or flu. Should you go to work or not? Do yourself and your coworkers a favor, particularly if one of your coworkers has AIDS: call in sick. Because of their compromised immune systems, PWAs are highly susceptible to contracting viruses of all kinds. Furthermore, contracting a cold or flu is more serious to PWAs than it is to relatively healthy people. For their sake, try to avoid PWAs when you have a contagious virus.

The same theory applies to public events, parties, meetings, and other social events. If you are sick, stay home unless your presence is essential. You'll be missed, but your thoughtfulness will be appreciated by PWAs.

39 When AIDS hits home

WHERE THERE'S A WILL . . .

You have just learned that either you or a loved one has tested positive for the HIV virus. You might be terrified. You might be angry. You might go into denial. But once you get over the initial shock and have had some time to think clearly, one of the first things you should do is to get your paperwork in order. If a friend or loved one has tested HIV positive, you should encourage and help him or her to do the same. The next few months or years might bring about a barrage of battles, and it is important that you and your loved ones be legally prepared for the onslaught.

The thought of "taking care of business" might be unpleasant, but it is altogether necessary, particularly for PWAs. PWAs have often been estranged from or disowned by their families. When the PWA becomes seriously ill, the family then steps in and dismisses his or her final wishes and sometimes his or her significant other.

Make out a last will and testament. If you die unmarried, it is quite likely that all of your possessions will become the property of your family unless you specify otherwise in a will. In addition to naming your beneficiaries in your will, you should name an executor. You can obtain a standard form for a will at most stationery and office supply stores. Simply fill out the form and sign it before witnesses and a notary public. Ideally, you should have a lawyer draw up the will. The fee is approximately $300. If you cannot afford this, call your local AIDS service organization and ask for help in drawing up the will.

You might also want to make out a living will. A living will describes what your wishes are should you find yourself in a particular medical situation and are unable to speak for yourself. A living will can relieve others from deciding what should be done in a serious situation—for example, whether you wish your life to be prolonged by artificial means. Although most states do not recognize a living will as a legal document, at least you will have made your wishes clear, and your loved ones will be relieved of the anguish of making those painful decisions for you.

If you have someone close to you whom you absolutely trust, consider filing a power-of-attorney document that would grant him or her the legal right to deal with your medical or financial matters. The person you designate as having power of attorney in your financial matters could write checks on your account, pay your bills, and so forth. The person you designate as having power of attorney in your medical matters could make important decisions regarding your medical treatment.

For the HIV-positive person, it cannot be stressed enough: Get your paperwork in order, *now*, while you are still healthy.

40 AIDS at the office

ALLEVIATE STRESS

It is imperative that PWAs avoid stress whenever possible. Stress has been proven to break down the immune system—something that PWAs, whose immune systems have already been decimated, cannot afford.

If you are an employer or even a co-worker of a PWA, try to avoid putting him or her in a stressful situation. One common result of AIDS is that it does help people put their priorities in perspective. Deadlines are important but life and death are more important in the long run.

You can help to alleviate a PWA's stress level outside the office as well by offering to help with the grocery shopping, the laundry, correspondence, and other errands. Remember, everyday things that are easy for you to do are often difficult or impossible for a PWA to do.

How can you tell if a PWA (or anyone, for that matter) is undergoing stress? The signs of stress include:

PHYSICAL
headaches
tight neck and shoulders
eye strain
sleep disorders
upset stomach
rash
hyperventilation

MENTAL/EMOTIONAL
depression
impatience
short-temper
disorientation
short attention span
difficulty with concentration

41 *In your spare time*

SHARE YOUR TALENTS

▸ If you're a doctor, offer your services to PWAs who can't afford medical care.

▸ If you're an attorney, offer your services to PWAs who have been discriminated against and can't afford legal representation.

▸ If you're a secretary, volunteer your office skills to your local AIDS organization.

▸ If you're a filmmaker, help produce movies or television shows that educate the public about AIDS and prompt compassion and understanding for PWAs.

▸ If you're an accountant, volunteer to help PWAs get their finances in order.

▸ If you speak more than one language, offer your services as a bilingual translator. Many PWAs could use your help!

Even if you can afford just one hour a week, donate that time to PWAs. There is something that everyone can do about AIDS. Be creative. There's a line from the musical *A Chorus Line,* which was directed by Michael Bennett, who died of AIDS in 1987: "I'm a dancer . . . a dancer dances." Do what *you* can do. Share *your* talents.

42 *Give unto others*

IT'S MY PARTY AND I'LL *TRY* IF I WANT TO!

Many birthday presents end up forgotten in a closet, unused or unworn. The next time you host a birthday party for yourself or for a friend, tell those invited that instead of bringing a present, they should bring a check made out to the local AIDS research or service organization of your choice. What better gift to give than the gift of life?

Of course, it doesn't have to be a birthday party. It can be a Christmas party, a wedding party, an anniversary party, or a housewarming party. After all, do you really need another punch bowl or decorative decanter? Instead of a housewarming, have a "heartwarming" instead by contributing funds as a group to the fight against AIDS.

43 *The ABCs of AIDS*

EMPOWER YOURSELF WITH INFORMATION

Obtain the U.S. Surgeon General's Report on AIDS. You can get a free copy (in either English or Spanish) by calling the National AIDS Information Clearinghouse at 1–800–342–2437.

44 AIDS at the office

FIGHT THE DISEASE, NOT THE PEOPLE WITH IT

What do you do about the co-worker who tells AIDS jokes, makes inflammatory anti-gay or anti-PWA remarks, or is just plain ignorant when it comes to AIDS?

The answer is simple. Find an especially informative article about AIDS, make a copy, and place it anonymously on the persons' desk. Or, if the person works in another office, FAX it to her or him. Let the person know that she or he needs help, that AIDS does not discriminate, that AIDS is not a vendetta against a segment of the population, and that no one is immune from the disease. Not even her or him. If you can't find an appropriate article to pass on, you can make a copy of the following article.

Los Angeles Times, June 6, 1991

A Family's AIDS Tragedy: 'It Can Happen to You'

By NORA ZAMICHOW
TIMES STAFF WRITER

CORONADO—Before Navy Lt. John Shaulis learned that his wife and son were infected, he believed that only homosexuals contracted the deadly disease AIDS—and that they deserved it.

"I was wrong," said Shaulis, 37. "It is torture—slow death. No one should suffer as my wife suffered. No one."

Shaulis, a Navy pilot, buried his wife, Linda, last week, three years after the death of the couple's 14-month-old son, August. Both were victims of AIDS.

Doctors believe that Linda Shaulis became infected during a sexual encounter years ago, in her college days. Unwittingly, she passed the virus along to her baby.

At her death, 32-year-old Linda Shaulis weighed 60 pounds and had gone blind.

"We are the perfect example of middle America," said Shaulis, who joined the Navy nine years ago. "If it happened to us, it can happen to you."

Acquired immune deficiency syndrome was first recognized as a disease 10 years ago this week by physicians with the Atlanta-based Centers for Disease Control.

> 'It is torture—slow death. No one should suffer as my wife suffered. No one.'
>
> LT. JOHN SHAULIS

Early in the AIDS epidemic, the disease was restricted largely to the homosexual community. But over the years, it has increasingly spilled into mainstream America. Linda Shaulis belonged to a small but growing number of women who contracted the virus through heterosexual activity.

As of April 30, there have been 174,893 AIDS cases nationwide, according to the Centers for Disease Control. Of those, 17,200 involve adult women, a third of whom contracted the virus that leads to the disease through heterosexual activity, health officials say.

Not everyone who has intercourse with an infected partner will be infected, experts say. In that way, Shaulis was lucky. He has not tested positive for HIV, the virus that causes AIDS.

At his wife's request, Shaulis kept her diagnosis a secret from most of his colleagues. Linda Shaulis also did not want her family to know. At her burial, all but one brother and sister believed that Linda died of cancer.

John Shaulis came to The Times to discuss his wife's death, hoping it might prevent further spread of the disease.

"I am 37, I've buried my wife, my son and I've got a headstone with my name—that's a little too early," Shaulis said. "This doesn't just happen to drug users or inner-city people. People think this doesn't happen in Coronado. But it does."

One year before her death, Linda Shaulis, a kindergarten teacher who grew up on a farm in a small Texas town, began keeping a diary. Originally, she bought the diary to write about John's life and hers, how they met, their hopes for the future.

Instead, she wrote about her death.

Reprinted by permission of the *Los Angeles Times*.

45 The ABCs of AIDS

AIDS AT SCHOOL: CLASS PROJECT

What can you do about AIDS if you are a junior high or high school student? Plenty! One good idea would be to organize a field trip to your local AIDS service organization. Another would be to find an articulate PWA and invite him or her to your class as a guest speaker. The PWA can talk to your fellow students about his or her experiences and answer questions that students might have about AIDS. It's one thing to read about a disease in a magazine or in a textbook; it's another thing entirely to meet someone with the disease face-to-face.

OTHER THINGS YOU CAN DO AT SCHOOL

- Organize a food drive and donate the collected goods to your local AIDS research or service organization.
- Work with your local hospital to organize a blood drive.
- Sponsor a car wash and donate the proceeds to your local AIDS research or service organization.
- Research and write about AIDS for a class project.

46 *In your spare time*

HUMANITARIAN GUINEA PIG

Volunteer to participate in an AIDS trial test. Every potential drug or treatment must be eventually tested on people who have tested positive for HIV.

If you are HIV negative, you can volunteer to participate in an AIDS vaccine test. A vaccine, of course, is administered to prevent a person from becoming infected and must be tested on people with normal, healthy immune systems.

Before volunteering for either a drug or a vaccine test, be sure you understand the possible risks and benefits of participating in such a test.

For more information on volunteering, contact:

- your local AIDS research organization
- your city or county health department
- the American Foundation for AIDS Research, 5900 Wilshire Blvd., 2nd floor, East Satellite, Los Angeles, CA 90036, 213/857-5900; or 40 W. 57th St., Ste. 406, New York, NY 10019, 212/333-3118
- NIAID Office of Communications, Bldg. #31, Room 7A32, 9000 Rockville Pike, Bethesda, MD 20892

47 The ABCs of AIDS

MEN: KEEP YOUR ROCKET IN YOUR POCKET

With AIDS, there are very few absolutes. Clearly, though, one of the best ways of reducing the risk of infection is to completely abstain from sex. However, for most sexually active people, this is an unrealistic option. People, by nature, are sexual.

So what can you do? Reduce your risk of infection by reducing the number of your sexual partners. A good rule of thumb is: When in doubt, don't. Or, for you men, "keep your rocket in your pocket."

More important, though, is that you practice safe sex *unfailingly* with the number of sexual partners that you do have.

48 *In your spare time*

CARE FOR THE CAREGIVER

Being the principal caregiver to a PWA is especially taxing, both emotionally and physically—a fact that is often forgotten or dismissed by society in general and by the PWA who is being cared for. But the greatest danger is when this fact is forgotten by the caregiver himself or herself.

The principal caregiver often lives with the PWA who he or she is caring for, and typically the caregiver has no private or personal time. Because of the considerable stress that he or she is constantly under, the caregiver often becomes stressed out, burned out, and sometimes physically sick. This is obviously not healthy for the caregiver or for the PWA.

What can you do? If you know a principal caregiver of a PWA, volunteer to occasionally substitute for him or her for an afternoon. Give the caregiver a much-needed and deserved break.

Or offer to take the caregiver out for a day. Encourage him or her to get a massage (perhaps given by you), to work out at the gym, or engage in other activities that will help to alleviate stress. It is equally important that you be there to *listen* to him or her. The caregiver's wants, needs, and feelings have probably been neglected since becoming a principal caregiver.

49 *The politics of AIDS*

MAGIC AND MAYHEM

There are two seconds left on the clock. The game is on the line. Earvin "Magic" Johnson has the ball and is playing the game of his life. Literally. On November 7, 1991, Magic Johnson announced to the world that he had contracted the AIDS virus. He further vowed to become a spokesperson for AIDS and went from being an N.B.A. superstar to being a U.S.A. national treasure of historic importance. There are numerous other public figures who have been and continue to be "heroes" in the face of the AIDS crisis. They have lent their names, their images, their time, and all of their resources to fighting this disease and the bigotry that unfortunately surrounds it.

Conversely, there are several public figures who have been and continue to be "villains" in the AIDS crisis. Some have used the media to espouse their homophobic remarks. Some have manipulated and used the disease to further their own political or personal ambitions. Some have publicly retracted their remarks following a wave of public furor; some have not.

What can you do? Support the heroes by going to their movies, watching their television shows, buying their records, and so forth. As for the villains, do *not* lend them your support or business. Furthermore, send them a note and let them know *why!* The following is a partial list and is subject to change.

CHEERS
   Cher
   Phil Donahue
   Faith Ford

Whoopi Goldberg
Elton John
Magic Johnson
Madonna
Bette Midler
Elizabeth Taylor
Jay Thomas

JEERS

Patrick Buchanan
Tom Clancy
Andrew Dice Clay
The Reverend Jerry Falwell
Sam Kinison
Andy Rooney
Axl Rose (Guns n' Roses)
The Reverend Lou Sheldon
The Reverend Donald Wildmon

SEND YOUR JEERS TO:

Patrick Buchanan
c/o *The Washington Times*
3600 New York Ave.
Washington, DC 20002

Tom Clancy
c/o Putnam Publishing
200 Madison Ave.
New York, NY 10016

Andrew Dice Clay
c/o Levine/Schneider Public Relations
8730 Sunset Blvd., 6th floor
Los Angeles, CA 90069

Jerry Falwell
c/o Thomas Road Baptist Church
701 Thomas Rd.
Lynchburg, VA 24502

Sam Kinison
c/o Triad Artists, Inc./Frank Rio
10100 Santa Monica Blvd., 16th floor
Los Angeles, CA 90067

Andy Rooney
c/o "60 Minutes"
524 W. 57th St.
New York, NY 10019

Axl Rose
c/o Geffen Records
9130 Sunset Blvd.
Los Angeles, CA 90069

The Reverend Lou Sheldon
c/o Traditional Values Coalition
100 S. Anaheim Blvd., #350
Anaheim, CA 92805

The Reverend Donald Wildmon
American Families Association
P.O. Drawer 2440
Tupelo, MS 38803

50 *The ABCs of AIDS*

TAKE THE TEST

What you don't know *can* hurt you. A few years ago, little could be done about AIDS medically and emotionally, so it didn't make much sense to take the HIV antibody test. Today, however, there are a variety of different treatments that have proven to be effective. There are no longer any excuses *not* to take the test. Protect yourself and protect those that you love. Get smart! Get tested!

Appendix A:

SAFE-SEX GUIDELINES

SAFE-SEX PRACTICES

- Hugging, massaging, touching
- Dry kissing
- Masturbation

LOW-RISK SEX PRACTICES

- French kissing (avoid if either partner has sores on or in the mouth)
- Mutual masturbation
- Vaginal intercourse using a condom
- Anal intercourse using a condom
- Oral sex (male) using a condom
- Oral sex (female) using a thin piece of latex between the mouth and the female organ (risk is increased during menstruation)
- Oral sex (involving the anus) using a thin piece of latex

UNSAFE-SEX PRACTICES

- Anal intercourse without a condom
- Vaginal intercourse without a condom
- Unprotected oral sex (male or female)
- Unprotected oral sex (anus)
- Unprotected penetration of the vagina with a hand or finger
- Unprotected penetration of the anus with a hand or finger
- Blood contact of any kind
- Sharing sex toys or needles

Appendix B:

THE AIDS GLOSSARY

You're trying to have a conversation about AIDS but you quickly become confused, and then disheartened, after being assaulted by a barrage of medical jargon. Don't give up. They are only words. The following is a simplified glossary to give you a better understanding of AIDS.

ACQUIRED IMMUNODEFICIENCY SYNDROME (AIDS)
A disease that breaks down the body's immune system, leaving it susceptible to opportunistic infections. A PWA has been stricken by one or more of these opportunistic infections and cancers that are not ordinarily a threat to people with healthy immune systems. In early 1992, the Centers for Disease Control in Atlanta is expected to expand the definition of AIDS to include people who are HIV positive and have a T-cell count of 200 or less. Although there is some controversy, it is commonly accepted that AIDS is caused by the HIV virus.

AIDS-RELATED COMPLEX (ARC)
Condition in which some of the symptoms (such as swollen lymph glands, night sweats, diarrhea, and fatigue) of AIDS have appeared, but the opportunistic infections associated with AIDS have not appeared.

ANTIBODY
A protein produced by the B-lymphocytes in the body to neutralize infections. With AIDS, these antibodies are usually rendered ineffective.

ANTIGEN
Substance or microorganism that the immune system recognizes as foreign and attempts to destroy.

ANTIVIRAL
Any drug that can destroy or weaken a virus, such as HIV.

AZT
Antiviral drug that is thought to be an effective treatment in prolonging the life of PWAs.

BACTRIM (AKA SEPTRA)
Effective treatment against pneumocystis carinii pneumonia.

CANDIDIASIS
Common yeast infection that can be an opportunistic infection associated with AIDS. It is sometimes referred to as "thrush" when found in the mouth or throat.

CARCINOMA
A form of skin cancer.

CO-FACTORS
Other infections or genetic predispositions that can increase the likelihood of HIV infection or the progression of a disease.

CRYPTOCOCCUS
A usually harmless fungus that causes meningitis and can be fatal to PWAs.

CRYPTOSPORIDIOSIS
Infection that can cause severe diarrhea, dehydration, and malnutrition in PWAs.

CYTOMEGALOVIRUS (CMV)
An opportunistic infection in the herpes family which is serious when associated with AIDS. In PWAs, CMV can cause diseases of the brain, eyes, lungs, and colon. CMV is also common in homosexual men who do not have AIDS.

DDC
Antiviral drug that has the potential to be a promising treatment in prolonging the life of PWAs.

DDI
Antiviral drug approved by the Food and Drug Administration in 1991 as an effective treatment in prolonging the life of PWAs.

ENCEPHALITIS
A disease or inflammation of the brain.

EPSTEIN-BARR VIRUS (EBV)
A herpes-like opportunistic infection that is serious when associated with AIDS. EBV causes one of two kinds of mononucleosis (the other is caused by CMV). It is transmitted by kissing and has been associated with Burkitt's lymphoma, a cancer of the lymph glands.

GAY-RELATED IMMUNODEFICIENCY DISEASE (GRID)
Obscure, early term for what is now called AIDS.

HEMOPHILIA
A genetic disease found almost exclusively in men in which the person's blood either does not clot or clots slowly. Hemophiliacs have been one of the high-risk groups most vulnerable to contracting AIDS through blood transfusions.

HERPES
This infection is exemplified by the eruption of painful blisters around the mouth or genital area and can be sexually transmitted. There are several viruses in the herpes family. All can be opportunistic infections associated with AIDS.

HERPES ZOSTER
The virus that causes shingles and chicken pox.

HODGKIN'S DISEASE
A form of cancer that affects the lymphatic system.

HUMAN IMMUNODEFICIENCY VIRUS (HIV)
The virus that is largely accepted (although there are some who disagree) to be the cause of AIDS. Also called HTLV-III/LAV (Human T-cell Lymphotropic Virus, type III).

IMMUNE SYSTEM
The bodily system, consisting of cells and proteins, that fights the infection of other organisms. In a PWA, the immune system is decimated.

INCUBATION PERIOD
The period between the initial infection and the first symptoms of disease.

KAPOSI'S SARCOMA (KS)
A rare form of cancer that is a frequently fatal opportunistic infection associated with AIDS. KS can manifest itself inside the body or as purplish lesions that appear on the legs or arms.

LYMPH NODES
Lymph nodes are located throughout the body and produce lymphocytes, a type of white blood cell. The most easily felt lymph nodes are found in the neck, armpits, and groin. Swollen lymph nodes indicate that there is infection being fought in the body.

LYMPHOCYTES
White blood cells in the blood and lymph fluid that are part of the body's immune system. These cells are invaded by HIV.

LYMPHOMA
A cancer of the lymphatic system.

MENINGITIS
An infection and inflammation of the membranes that cover the brain and spinal cord.

MYCOBACTERIUM AVIUM INTRACELLULARE (MAI)
A Mycobaterium that lives in and infects the respiratory tract. In AIDS patients the infection is almost always disseminated, infecting many areas of the body. It has been found to cause serious illness in PWAs. MAI is widespread in the environment, probably in the soil, and is not spread from person to person.

OPPORTUNISTIC INFECTIONS
Infections that lie dormant in the body until the immune system is seriously compromised. Sensing the opportunity, the infections overwhelm the immune system. In conjunction with HIV, the infections become life threatening.

PENTAMIDINE
A drug used against pneumocystis carinii pneumonia.

PNEUMOCYSTIS CARINII PNEUMONIA (PCP)
Pneumonia that is one of the most common and deadly opportunistic infections associated with AIDS.

RETROVIRUS
A virus that contains RNA, not DNA, as its genetic material. The AIDS virus, HIV, is a retrovirus.

T-HELPER LYMPHOCYTES (T-4 CELLS)
White blood cells in the body which are integral to the fight against invading organisms.

THRUSH
An infection in the mouth, tongue, and throat caused by candida fungus.

TOXOPLASMOSIS
A disease that is rarely a threat to those with healthy immune systems. In PWAs, however, toxoplasmosis can cause brain damage and can be fatal.

Appendix C:

DIRECTORY OF AIDS SERVICE AND RESEARCH ORGANIZATIONS

NATIONAL

National AIDS Hotline
1–800–342–AIDS (English)
1–800–344–SIDA (Spanish)

AIDS Action Council
2033 M St., N.W., Ste. 801
Washington, DC 20036
202/293–2886

American Foundation for AIDS Research (AmFAR)
1515 Broadway, #3601
New York, NY 10036
212/719–0033

or

5900 Wilshire Blvd., 2nd Floor
East Satellite
Los Angeles, CA 90036
213/857–5900

Centers for Disease Control
404/639–3311

Coalition of Hispanic Health & Human Services Organizations
1030 15th St., N.W.
Washington, DC 20005
202/371–2100

Mothers of AIDS Patients
P.O. Box 81082
San Diego, CA 92128
619/234–3432

or

P.O. Box 1763
Lomita, CA 90717–9998
213/530–2109

National AIDS Information Clearinghouse
P.O. Box 6003
Rockville, MD 20850
1–800–458–5231; 1–800–342–2437

National AIDS Network
729 Eighth Street, S.E., #300
Washington, DC 20003
202/546–2424

National Gay Task Force
AIDS Information Hotline:
1–800–221–7044

CONTACT YOUR LOCAL AIDS SERVICE ORGANIZATION

ALABAMA

AIDS Hotline: 1–800–228–0469

Birmingham AIDS Outreach
2503 Eleventh Ave. South
Birmingham, AL 35205
205/322–0757

Mobile AIDS Support System:
205/433–6277

Montgomery AIDS Outreach:
205/284–2273

ALASKA

AIDS Hotline: 1–800–478–AIDS

Alaskan AIDS Assistance
Association
417 W. Eighth Ave.
Anchorage, AK 99501
907/276–4880

Anchorage, AIDS Project:
907/276–4880; 1–800–248–AIDS

ARIZONA

AIDS Hotline: 1–800–334–1540

Aids Information Line:
602/234–2752

Arizona AIDS Project
736 E. Flynn St.
Phoenix, AZ 85014
602/277–1929; 602/277–1961
(Hotline)

Arizona Stop AIDS Project
919 N. First St.
Phoenix, AZ 85014
602/420–9396

Tucson AIDS Project
151 S. Tucson Blvd., #252
Tucson, AZ 85716
602/322–6226; 602/326–AIDS or
602/326–2437 (Hotline)

ARKANSAS

AIDS Hotline: 1–800–445–7720

Arkansas AIDS Foundation
P.O. Box 5007
Little Rock AR 72225
501/663–7833

CALIFORNIA

Northern California Hotline:
1–800–367–2437

Southern California Hotline:
1–800–922–2437

Northern California

AIDS Project of the East Bay
565 16th St.
Oakland, CA 94612
415/834–8181

Ellipse
2121 S. El Camino Real, #505
San Mateo, CA 94403
415/572–9702

Gay Men's Health Collective
2339 Durant
Berkeley, CA 94704
415/644–0425

Sacramento AIDS Foundation
1900 K St., #201
Sacramento, CA 95814
916/448–AIDS

San Francisco AIDS Foundation
25 Van Ness Ave., #660
San Francisco, CA 94102
415/864–5855; 415/864–4376;
1–800–FOR–AIDS

Shanti Project
525 Howard St.
San Francisco, CA 94105
415/777–2273

Sonoma County AIDS Network
Face to Face
P.O. Box 1599
Guerneville, CA 95446
707/887–1581

Southern California

Aid for AIDS
8235 Santa Monica Blvd., #200
West Hollywood, CA 90046
213/656–1107

AIDS Project Los Angeles
6721 Romaine St.
Los Angeles, CA 90036
213/962–1600; 213/876–AIDS;
1–800–922–AIDS

Bakersfield AIDS Hotline:
1–800–367–2437

Being Alive
4222 Santa Monica Blvd.
Los Angeles, CA 90026
213/667–3262

CORE Program
7740 1/2 Santa Monica Blvd.
West Hollywood, CA 90046
213/656-8201

Gay & Lesbian Community Service Center
12832 Garden Grove Blvd. A
Garden Grove, CA 92643
714/534–0862 (front desk)
714/534–3261 (crisis line)
714/534–0961 (AIDS Response Program)

Long Beach Dept. of Health AIDS Office
2655 Pine Ave.
Long Beach, CA 90806
213/427–7421

Minority AIDS Project
5149 Jefferson Blvd.
Los Angeles, CA 90016
213/936–4949

Project AHEAD
1936A E. Fourth
Long Beach, CA 90802
213/590–9019

Project Angel Food
650 N. Robertson Blvd.
Los Angeles, CA 90069
310/850-0877

San Diego AIDS Project
3777 Fourth Ave.
San Diego, CA 92103
619/543–0300; 619/543–0604

Shanti Foundation
6855 Santa Monica Blvd., #408
Los Angeles, CA 90046
213/962–8197

Women's AIDS Project
8235 Santa Monica Blvd., #201
West Hollywood, CA 90046
213/650–1508

COLORADO

AIDS Hotline: 1–800–252–2437

AIDS Hotline: 303/333–4336

Boulder County AIDS Project
303/837–0166

Colorado AIDS Project
1576 Sherman
Denver, CO 80203
303/837–0166

Denver Catholic Community Services
Hospice of Peace
200 Josephine St.
Denver, CO 80206
303/388–4435

CONNECTICUT

AIDS Hotline: 203/566–1157

AIDS Project New Haven
254 College St. #200
New Haven, CT 06511
203/624–0947;
203/624–AIDS (Hotline)

AIDS Project of Greater Danbury
P.O. Box 91
Bethel, CT 06801
203/426–5626;
203/797–7900 (Hotline)

Northwest Connecticut AIDS Project
P.O. Box 985
Torrington, CT 06790
203/482–1596;
203/567–4111 (Hotline)

DELAWARE

AIDS Hotline: 1–800–422–0429

AIDS Program Office
302/995–8422

DISTRICT OF COLUMBIA

AIDS Information: 202/332–AIDS

LifeLink
2025 Eye St., N.W., #417
Washington, DC 20006
202/833–3070

Whitman-Walker Clinic
1407 S St., N.W.
Washington, DC 20009
202/797–3500; 202/332–2437 or
202/332–3926 (Hotline)

FLORIDA

AIDS Hotline: 1–800–FLA–AIDS

Center One/AID
P.O. Box 8152
Ft. Lauderdale, FL 33310
305/561–0807; 305/485–7175;
1–800–325–5371 (Hotline)

Health Crisis Network
1351 N.W. 20th St.
Miami, FL 33242
305/326–8833; 1–800–443–5046;
305/324–5148 or 305/634–4636
(Hotline)

Key West AIDS Help, Inc.
305/296–6196

North Central Florida AIDS Network
1005-I S.E. Fourth Ave.
Gainesville, FL 32601
904/372–4370

Orlando AIDS Unified Resources, Inc.
407/849–1452

Tampa AIDS Network
813/221–6420

GEORGIA

AIDS Hotline: 1–800–551–2728

AIDS Atlanta
1132 W. Peachtree St., N.W., #102
Atlanta, GA 30309
404/872–0600; 1–800–551–2728;
404/876–9944 (Hotline)

AIDS Crisis Volunteers
2623 Washington Rd., #101-E
Augusta, GA 30904
404/733–9000

HAWAII

AIDS HOTLINE: 1–800–922–2437

AIDS Foundation of Hawaii
P.O. Box 88980
Honolulu, HI 96830
808/924–2437

Gay Community Center
1154 Fort St. Mall, #415
Honolulu, HI 96801
808/536–6000

Honolulu Life Foundation
808/971–2437

IDAHO

AIDS Hotline: 1–800–833–AIDS

Boise AIDS Foundation
208/345–2277

State AIDS Program
208/334–5930

ILLINOIS

AIDS Hotline: 1–800–243–2438

AIDS Foundation of Chicago
2035 N. Lincoln Ave.
Chicago, IL 60614
312/525–9466

Chicago AIDS Comprehensive Center
312/908–9191

Chicago AIDS Foundation
312/642–5454

Madison County AIDS Prevention Program
1254 Niedringhaus Ave.
Granite, IL 62040
618/452–1380; 1–800–345–2383 (Hotline)

INDIANA

State Office of AIDS Activity:
317/633–0851

Bag Ladies
P.O. Box 441211
Indianapolis, IN 46224
317/632–0123

Catholic Social Services
919 Fairfield Ave.
Ft. Wayne, IN 46802
219/422–7511

Fort Wayne AIDS Task Force:
219/424–0844

Indianapolis AIDS Task Force:
317/634–1441; 317/257–HOPE

Shalico Center
1106 Meridian Plaza #555
Anderson, IN 46016
317/646–9206

IOWA

AIDS HOTLINE: 1-800-532-3301

Central Iowa AIDS Project
c/o American Red Cross
515/243-7681; 1-800-445-AIDS (Hotline)

KANSAS

AIDS Hotline: 1-800-232-0040

Topeka AIDS Project:
913/232-3100

Wichita AIDS Referral Services:
316/264-2437

KENTUCKY

AIDS Hotline: 1-800-654-AIDS

AIDS Crisis Task Force
P.O. Box 11442
Lexington, KY 40575
606/281-5151

Louisville-Jefferson County Board of Health
AIDS Prevention Office
502/625-5601

North Kentucky AIDS Task Force:
606/291-0770

LOUISIANA

AIDS Hotline New Orleans:
504/522-2437

Baton Rouge AIDS Task Force:
504/923-2277

Central Louisiana AIDS Support Services
1771 Elliott St. B
Alexandria, LA 71301
318/442-1010

New Orleans AIDS Project
1231 Prytania St.
New Orleans, LA 70130
504/523-3755

New Orleans AIDS Task Force:
504/891-3732

MAINE

AIDS Hotline: 207/775-1267

AIDS Hotline: 1-800-851-2437

AIDS Project Portland
48 Deering St.
Portland, ME 04104
207/774-6877; 207/775-1267; 1-800-851-AIDS

MARYLAND

AIDS Hotline: 1-800-638-6252

AIDS Interfaith Network
210 W. Madison St.
Baltimore, MD 21201
301/728-5545

Baltimore Health Education & Resource Organization (HERO):
301/685-1180; 1-800-638-6252

MASSACHUSETTS

AIDS Hotline: 1-800-235-2331

AIDS Action Committee
131 Clarendon St.
Boston, MA 02116
617/437-6200

AIDS Project Worcester
51 Jackson St.
Worcester, MA 01609
508/755-3773

MICHIGAN

AIDS Hotline: 1-800-872-AIDS

Community Health & Awareness Group
3028 E. Grand Blvd.
Detroit, MI 48202
313/872-2424

Wellness House of Michigan
P.O. Box 03827
Detroit, MI 48203
313/342-1230

MINNESOTA

AIDS Hotlines: 612-870-0700; 1-800-248-AIDS

Minnesota AIDS Project
2025 Nicollett Ave. South, #200
Minneapolis, MN 55044
612/870-7773

MISSISSIPPI

State AIDS Hotline:
1-800-826-2961

Mississippi Gay Alliance
P.O. Box 8342
Jackson, MI 32904
601/353-7611

MISSOURI

AIDS Hotline: 1-800-533-2437

St. Louis Effort For AIDS
4050 Lindell Blvd.
St. Louis, MO 63108
314/531-2847; 314/531-7400 (Hotline)

MONTANA

AIDS Hotline: 1-800-537-6187

Billings AIDS Support Network
P.O. Box 1748
Billings, MT 59103
406/245-2029; 405/252-1212

NEBRASKA

AIDS Hotlines: 1-800-432-7514; 1-800-782-2437

Nebraska AIDS Project
3624 Leavenworth St.
Omaha, NE 68105
402/342-4233

NEVADA

AIDS Hotline: 1-800-842-AIDS

AID for AIDS of Nevada
2211 S. Maryland Parkway
Las Vegas, NV 89104
702/369-6162

Reno, Nevada, AIDS Foundation:
702/329-2437

NEW HAMPSHIRE

AIDS Hotline: 1-800-872-8909

Feminist Health Care Center of Portsmouth
STD Clinic
232 Court St.
Portsmouth, NH 03801
603/436-7588

Manchester, AIDS Foundation:
603/595-0218

NEW JERSEY

AIDS Hotline: 1-800-624-2377

Hyacinth Foundation
211 Livingston Ave.
New Brunswick, NJ 08901
201/246-8439; 1-800-433-0254

Newark Lesbian & Gay AIDS Awareness:
201/763-2919

NEW MEXICO

AIDS HOTLINE: 1-800-545-AIDS

AIDS Prevention Program
1190 South St. Francis Dr.
Santa Fe, NM 87503
505/827-0090

New Mexico AIDS Services
129 W. San Francisco
Santa Fe, NM 87108
505/984-0911

New Mexico AIDS Services
124 Quincy, N.E.
Albuquerque, NM 87108
505/266-0911

Southwest AIDS Committee
P.O. Box 6850
Las Cruces, NM 88006
505/525-AIDS

NEW YORK

AID Hotline: 1-800-462-1884

AIDS Council of NENY
307 Hamilton St.
Albany, NY 12210
518/434-4686; 518/445-AIDS (Hotline)

AIDS Rochester
20 University Ave.
Rochester, NY 14605
716/232-3580;
716/232-4430 (Hotline)

Gay Men's Health Crisis
129 West 20th St.
New York, NY 10011
212/807-6664;
212/807-6655 (Hotline)

Western New York AIDS Program
220 Delaware, #512
Buffalo, NY 14202
716/847-2441;
716/847-2437 (Hotline)

NORTH CAROLINA

AIDS Hotline: 1-800-342-2437

Metrolina AIDS Project
1801 Fifth St.
Charlotte, NC 28204
704/333-2437; 704/333-1435

Raleigh AIDS Control Program:
919/733-7301

NORTH DAKOTA

AIDS Hotline: 1-800-472-2180

OHIO

AIDS Hotline: 1-800-332-2437

Canton AIDS Task Force:
216/489-3231

Cincinnati Ambrose Clement Health Clinic:
513/352-3139

Cleveland Health Issues Task Force:
216/621-0766

Columbus AIDS Task Force
1500 W. Third, #329
Columbus, OH 43212
614/488–2437; 614/645–2437

OKLAHOMA

AIDS Hotline: 1–800–522–9054

Oklahoma City Oasis Community Center:
405/525–AIDS

Tulsa Shanti:
918/749–7898

OREGON

AIDS Hotline: 1–800–777–2437

Cascade AIDS Project
408 S.W. Second, #412
Portland, OR 97204
503/223–5907

Oregon AIDS Task Force:
503/226–6678

PENNSYLVANIA

AIDS Hotline: 1–800–692–7254

Philadelphia AIDS Task Force
1216 Walnut
Philadelphia, PA 19107
215/545–8686; 215/732–AIDS

RHODE ISLAND

AIDS Hotline: 1–800–726–3010

Rhode Island Project AIDS
22 Hayes St.
Providence, RI 02908
401/277–6545; 401/277–6502;
401/831–5522

SOUTH CAROLINA

AIDS Hotline: 1–800–322–AIDS

Carolina AIDS Research and Education:
803/777–2273

Palmetto AIDS Life Support Services
P.O. Box 12124
Columbia, SC 29211
803/779–7257;
1–800–868–PALS (Hotline)

SOUTH DAKOTA

AIDS Hotline: 1–800–592–1861

Public Health Center
1320 S. Minnesota Ave.
Sioux Falls, SD 57105
605/335–5020

TENNESSEE

AIDS Hotline: 1–800–525–2437

Aid to End AIDS Committee
689 Melrose
Memphis, TN 38104
901/458–2437

Chattanooga Cares:
615/265–2273; 615/757–2745

Knoxville AIDS Response:
615/523–AIDS

Nashville CARES
P.O. Box 25107
Nashville, TN 37202
615/385–1510;
615/385–AIDS (Hotline)

TEXAS

State AIDS Hotline:
1-800-248-1091

AIDS Foundation Houston
3927 Essex Lane, #1155
Houston, TX 77027
713/623-6796; 713/524-AIDS

AIDS Services of Austin
P.O. Box 4874
202 W. 17th St.
Austin, TX 78765
512/472-2273; 512/472-AIDS

Coastal Bend AIDS Foundation
616 S. Tancahua
Corpus Christi, TX 78401
512/883-5815; 512/883-CARE

Dallas AIDS Resource Center:
214/521-5124; 214/559-AIDS

West Texas AIDS Foundation
P.O. Box 93120
Lubbock, TX 79493
806/747-2437

UTAH

AIDS Hotline: 1-800-537-1046

Utah AIDS Foundation
P.O. Box 3373
Salt Lake City, UT 84110
801/531-8238; 1-800-FON-AIDS

VERMONT

AIDS Hotline: 1-800-882-AIDS

Vermont CARES
30 Elmwood Ave.
Burlington, VT 05402
802/863-AIDS

VIRGINIA

AIDS Hotline: 1-800-533-4148

Tidewater AIDS Crisis Task Force
814 W. 41st St.
Norfolk, VA 23508
804/423-5859

WASHINGTON

AIDS Hotline: 1-800-272-AIDS

Northwest AIDS Foundation
1818 E. Madison
Seattle, WA 98122
206/329-6923;
206/587-4999 (Hotline)

Olympia AIDS Task Force:
206/352-2375

WEST VIRGINIA

AIDS Hotline: 1-800-642-8244

WISCONSIN

AIDS Hotline: 1-800-334-AIDS

Madison AIDS Support Network
23 N. Pickney
Madison, WI 53703
608/255-1711

Milwaukee AIDS Project
315 W. Court St.
Milwaukee, WI 53212
414/273-2437

WYOMING

AIDS Hotline: 1-800-327-3577

Wyoming AIDS Project
P.O. Box 9353
Casper, WY 82609
307/237-7833

Parting thoughts...

*AIDS is no longer a disease
of women and men.
AIDS is a disease of families.*

—UNITED STATES SURGEON GENERAL ANTONIA NOVELLO
September 1991

*Out nation's leaders have not done well.
[The White House] has rarely broken
its silence [on AIDS].*

—THE NATIONAL COMMISSION ON AIDS
September 1991

*And so, my fellow Americans:
ask not what your country can do for you—
ask what you can do for your country.*

—JOHN FITZGERALD KENNEDY
January 1961